"Tribal Perspectives"

of the

Tübatulabal Baskets

in the

California State Parks Museum Resource Center

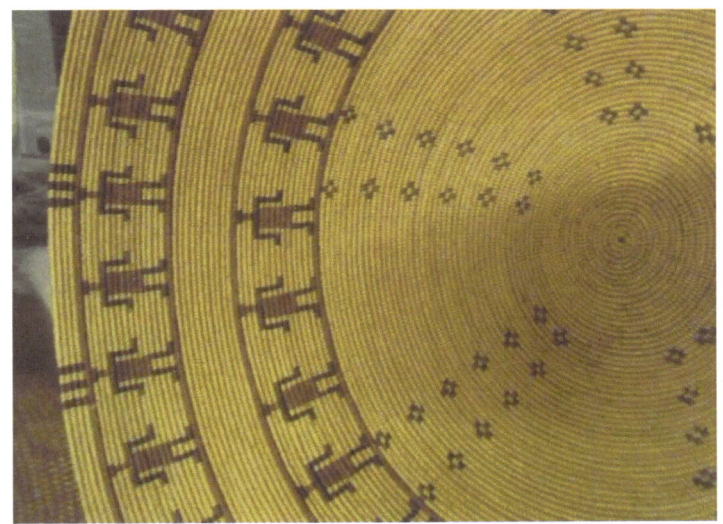

Tübatulabal Tribe

1st Edition, December 2011
Published by Tübatulabal Tribe
Written by Dr. Donna Miranda-Begay
Mountain Mesa, California 93240

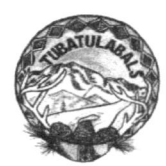

ISBN-13: 978-1467996365
ISBN-10: 146799636X

Dedication and Contribution

This book is dedicated to our Tübatulabal "Basket Maker Ancestors" who dedicated their lives in both the "life" and art of traditional basket making. They knew when to harvest for their basket materials and shared their patterns with neighboring Tribes.

In this book, the Tübatulabal Tribe and Pakanapul Language Program offer their Tribal perspectives of their basket designs and traditional uses. We thank the Pakanapul Language Program and the Tübatulabal Tribe Tribal Office for their guidance with the contents and cultural meaning of this book.

This is our Tribe's first edition of this book. There will be additional books based on future tours of the Smithsonian in Washington, D.C., Phoebe Hearst Museum in Berkeley, CA, University of California Los Angeles, and other museums where more Tübatulabal baskets are currently located.

Appreciation to the following people who contribute and shared their knowledge and traditional language for this book:

Brian Bibby	Betsy Johnson
Sherry Click	Virgie Russell
Bertha Eller	Dale Johnson
Anthony Stone	Lindsay Marean
Marie Bovey	Samantha Riding-Red-Horse
Robert Gomez	William Otay, Sr.
Dr. Martha Macri	Dr. "Dotty" Theodoratus
Karen Blom	Louise Miranda-Akers

Table of Contents

Baskets at the California State Parks Archives

In December 2009, Tübatulabal (Tuh-bah-tuh-la-bal) Tribe's Tribal Chairwoman "timiwal" Dr. Donna Miranda-Begay and Tribal Member - Marie Bovey met with California State Parks Museum

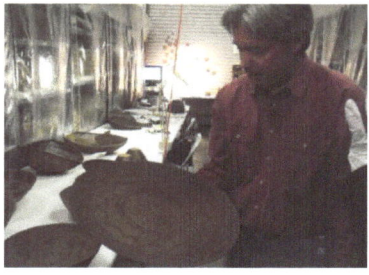

Resource Center's Consultant Brian Bibby (pictured to the right). Brian is a scholar and researcher who has met and worked many years with California Tribes, California Tribal Basket Makers, and California State Parks Museums. Brian has developed many public exhibits of California Tribal Baskets for museums, universities, and other public institutions. Our Tribe scheduled an appointment with Brian who provided a tour and overview of our Tübatulabal Baskets.

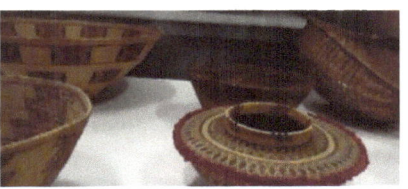

The baskets discussed in this book are stored at the California State Parks Museum Resource Center in a secure and climate controlled environment. There are about 4,000 Baskets (approximately, 3,000 being California Tribal baskets) located at this facility.

Many historic Tribal baskets have traveled very interesting journeys. Through correspondence, Brian Bibby describes the Hall-Sheedy collection (which include Tübatulabal baskets) travel route. Charles P. Wilcomb had purchased Tribal baskets in the late 1800's. Mr. Wilcomb was known to make purchases in the field – directly from Tribal people. Mr. Wilcomb planned to sell these Tribal baskets to deYoung Museum in San Francisco. However, Mr. deYoung would not reimburse Wilcomb for these baskets. As a result, these baskets were sold (about 1905) to wealthy collector in Pennsylvania, Robert Hall. Robert Hall had a museum built within his summer residence. Mr. Hall hired Wilcom to come and take care of the collection. Later, in 1908, Wilcomb accepted a job to be curator of the new Oakland Museum. He worked there until his death in 1915. The collection owned by Robert Hall, ended up in Southern California with Mr. Hall's grandson, Mr. Sheedy. Through Mr. Sheedy's donation, the "Hall-Sheedy" basket collection came to State Parks in the late 1960's (Bibby, 2010).

There are 18 Tübatulabal baskets at the California State Parks Museum Resource Center. We appreciate the time and effort of Brian's work to help identify the basket materials, linkages to Tribe(s), cultural meaning, age of basket and basket's place of origin.

Tübatulabal Tribe History

According to documented sources (Wheeler-Voegelin, 1938 and Smith, 1978) and members of our Tribe, the Tübatulabals have always occupied the lower regions of the Southern Sierra Nevada surrounding the North and South Forks of the Kern River. The habitat area of the tribe is comprised of approximately 1,300 square miles of the Kern River as it rushes down the Sierra Nevada Mountains from Mt. Whitney.

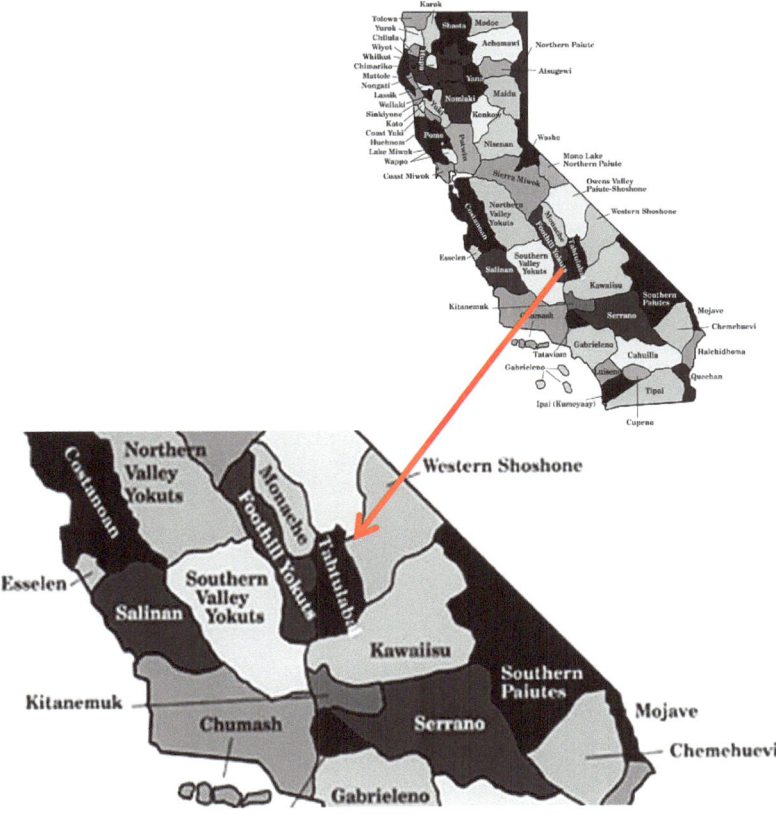

Figure 1 - Map from California Indian Library Collection

The Tübatulabal traditional territory included the Kern and South Fork Kern Rivers drainages extending from very high mountainous terrain in the north to about 41 miles below the junction of the two rivers in the south. The high mountains in the north (2,500 to 14,500 feet) are interspersed with lakes and meadows. The southern area (2,500 to 3,000 feet) has three connected valleys: Kern Valley, South Fork Kern Valley, and Hot Springs Valley where summers are hot and winters cold and rainy. The valleys are grasslands and chaparral with cacti, scrub oaks, willows, elderberry, and cottonwoods as primary vegetation with some joshua trees, junipers, piñons, oaks, and sugar pines. (Theodoratus & McBride, 2009).

According to tribal myth, the deep crags, crevices, and crooks of the canyon moving upward (east from the mouth of the Kern Canyon) to the upper reaches of the Kern River were "created by hawk and duck as they bounced back and forth, to and from along the canyon walls as they raced up the river" (Waterman, n.d.),

The valley of the Kern River has been the home of three distinct bands which are collectively named Tübatulabal. The name Tübatulabal (which is loosely translated as "Pine-nut Eaters or Gatherers") has been appended to the tribe by their neighbors to the west (Yokuts). At one point in history the Yokuts also called the Tübatulabals, "Pitanisha" (place where the rivers fork).

The three bands that comprise the Tübatulabal Tribe are the Palegawan (Kern Canyon to Bakersfield), Pakanapul (Mount Whitney to Lake Isabella to Ridgecrest), and Bankalachi "Toloim" (Greenhorn

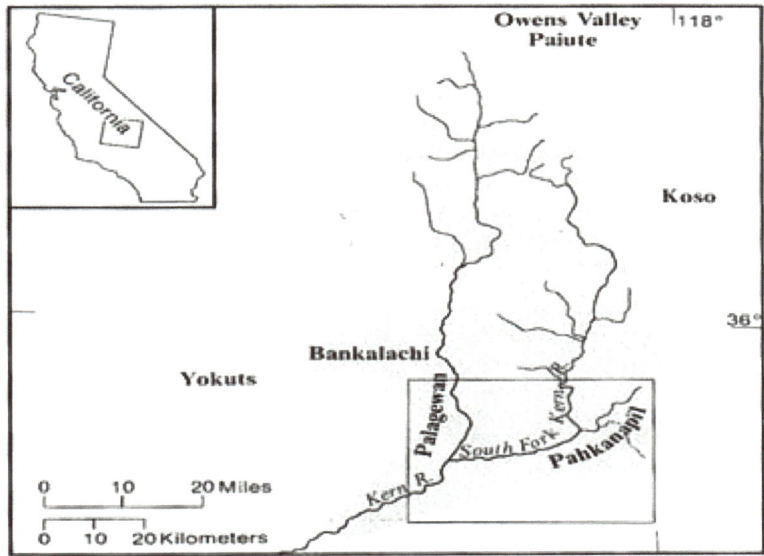

Figure 2 – Tübatulabal Tribal Territory map (Voegelin 1938:42)

Mountains and Poso Flats). They are culturally and linguistically closely related. The Pakanapul is the only band which has, to some degree, survived European transgression and occupancy.

The name for the north fork of the river has the Indian name of Palegewanap or "place of the big river". The south fork of the river conversely was given the name of "kutchibichwanap palap" or "place of the little river" (Gomez, 2009).

Language of the Tübatulabal Tribe

Tübatulabal is a Uto-Aztecan language that, although definitely part of the Uto-Aztecan stock, is not closely related to other languages in that group. Located in the Kern Valley, the Tübatulabal people had contact with the Yokuts to the north and west, as well as to Numic groups to the east. On their southern border, the Tübatulabal had ties with Kitanemuk, Serrano, and Tataviam People who spoke the Takic branch of Uto-Aztecan. The Tübatulabal were significant participants and go-betweens in the trade networks connecting the Great Basin, the southern deserts, the Central Valley, and the coastal groups (Macri, 2009).

The Tübatulabal Pakanapul band speaks the "paka'anil" dialect (note: no upper case in paka'anil dialect). This dialect will be used in this book to help describe the baskets' designs and meaning.

The Pakanapul Language program provided the following basket related descriptions: English – "paka'anil spelling" (phonetic spelling):

Basket ladle – "hom'mobit" (home-mo-bit): this is a ladle used to help sift acorns or piñon nuts and loosen seeds from plants.

Burden basket cap – "waaniht" (waa-neet): burden basket caps used for both work and ceremonies.

Coiled / twined – "cüül" (shuul): coiled and twined basket weaving techniques that were very common in our baskets.

Cooking basket – "hom'mol" (home-mole): tightly woven basket used with cooking rocks.

Deer grass – "masil" (ma-seal): deer grass is harvested when it is green and soaked in water just prior to weaving into a basket. "masil" can also be used to make twine.

Deer hoof – "culunt tohiil" (shu-lunt toe-hill): deer hoof pattern is very symmetrical and reflects animal spirit and method of travel or direction.

Flat sifter – "waat" (waht): flat and round basket used in ceremonies and times of "big time" or fiestas (larger community gatherings). The baskets were also used by our Medicine people or Shamans in shooting contest.

King snake –" pok poogonooloowun" (poke-poo-go-noo-low-wun): the King snake is good and helps to keep the rattlesnake away. Never hurt a King snake.

Little boy – "anaihiiloowun" (an-eye-he-low-wun): the little boy design represents a person, people, or community.

Meal basket – "po' nol" (poo-nol): this basket was used to serve food.

Money basket – "ukuluct" (uk-kuu-lust): this basket was used to store traditional money, valuable shells, and stones.

Peeled shoot of red bud – "kadaadihpul" (ka-daa-dee-pul): red bud blooms in March/April and after the bloom season red bud can be harvested for basket making and also for making tea (helps with common cold and sore throat). Note: Never harvest a native plant during its blooming season – the plant will not offer the same strength, could be poisonous, not ready for mature use or flavor, or may not produce for the next season.

Quail – "takaah" (ta-kah): quail is very common bird in Kern Valley. Quail is used for both food and basket making uses. The quail tail feathers are used as fringe for bottle neck and money jar baskets.

Rattlesnake –"tsümindingloowün" (sue-mung-ting-low-wun): the rattlesnake brings us water and is respected. Never talk about animals in a bad way – they can hear you and talk with each other. The backs of rattlesnakes have diamond and symmetrical patterns that are reflected in the Tübatulabal baskets.

Red bud – "kadaadihpul" (kah-dah-dee-pull): a bush with brown/burgundy stems often used in Tübatulabal baskets.

Thunder – "dawaagalanggil" (da-wog-ga-long-ill): this symbol represents new beginning and very active spirits of the sky .

Overall, Tübatulabal baskets are barely distinguishable from Yokuts . Tübatulabal baskets have a finer weave compared to Yokut baskets. The majority of the time Tübatulabal baskets were used by women, however, the men would trap fish with a fishing basket.

Tübatulabal Basket Makers

Louisa Francisco, a "Bankalachi" was well known for her wonderful baskets. Some of our Tübatulabal families in Kern Valley are related to Louisa. Many of our ancestors married into the Tule River Indians, Tachi Yokuts, and Tejon Tribes. Our Tribal families shared in their basket making designs, materials, and weaving techniques.

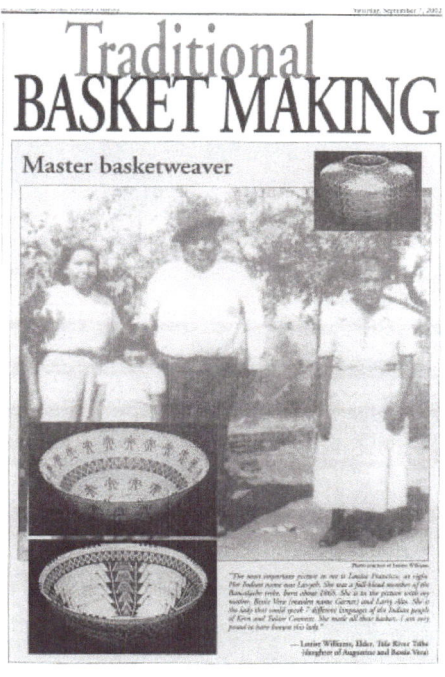

"The most important picture to me is Louisa Francisco, at right. Her Indian name was Las-yeh. She was a full-blood member of the Bancalache tribe, born about 1865. She is in the picture with my mother, Bessie Vera (maiden name Garner) and Larry Alto. She is the lady that could speak 7 different languages of the Indian people of Kern and Tulare Counties. She made all these baskets. I am very proud to have known this lady."

— Louise Williams, Elder, Tule River Tribe
(daughter of Augustine and Bessie Vera)

Louisa had a brother name Peter, both came from Poso Flat – a Bankalachi (Toloim) Village. Louisa was born January 9, 1865 at Poso Flat (Kern County) and died at age 95 in 1954. She was living on the Tule River Indian Reservation just prior to her death.

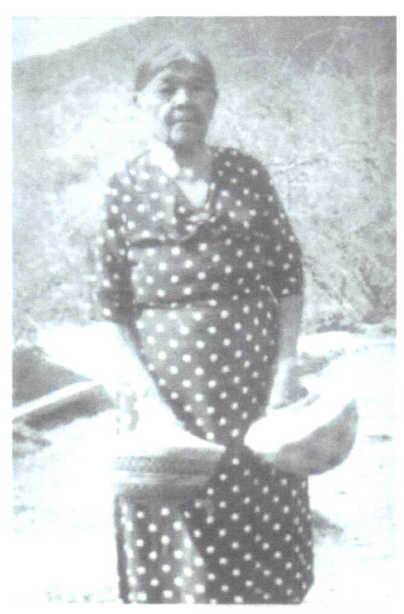

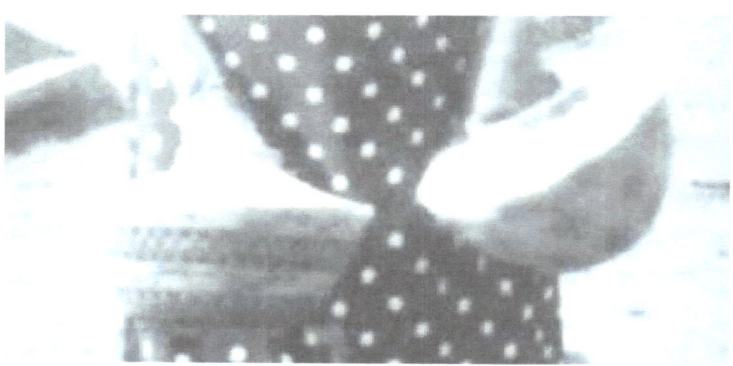

Estefana Miranda, a Pakanapul, lived in Weldon, CA (born January 13, 1895 and died in 1957) on the Miranda Allotment (IND 14). Estefana was the daughter of Steban Miranda (a Tübatulabal Chief "timiwal"). Estefana knew how to harvest native tobacco, acorns, salt grass, and other native foods of the South Fork of Kern Valley and Kelso Valley areas. She knew how to make "flat round" basket used for both sifting and

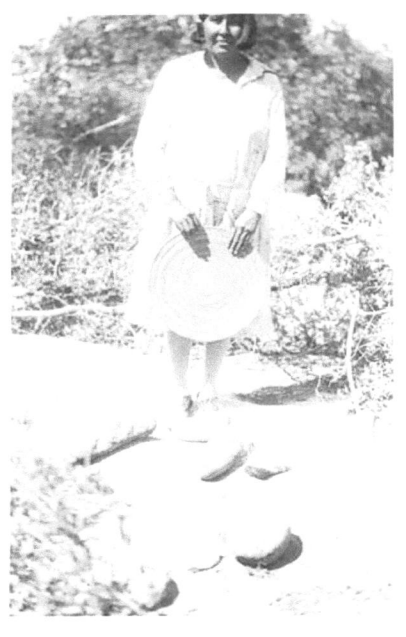

ceremonies. Her baskets were also used to process piñon nuts and acorns picked from Walker Pass, Kennedy Meadows, and Greenhorn Mountain areas. A Tübatulabal Elder, William Otay (92 years old), who lived in Weldon, CA next to the South Fork of the Kern River in 1920's remembers Estefana and shares this story: "Estefana would ride her horse from the Miranda Allotment to Kernville. On her way to Kernville, she would pass by our house and say hello. As Estefana left our house on her horse, we would watch her make her horse jump back and forth across the dirt ditches. She was a good horseman." (Otay, 2009).

It is also important to note that during the late 1800's through early 1900s, California Indian baskets were bought by both private and public buyers who would sell baskets to museums or trading stores. Today, many of these baskets have been placed into museums.

Tübatulabal Traditional Uses of Their Baskets

Sifting ladle basket -"hom'mobit" (home-mo-bit): this basket was used to sift acorns and piñon nut shells and also as a seed beater (help loosen seeds from plants into burden basket). This basket is made of willow branches (Wilcom collected basket in Kernville, about 1898-1902).

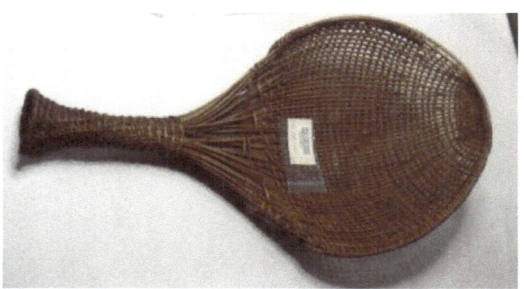

Large sifting basket – this basket would be used for processing large batches of cracked acorns, piñon nuts, and salt grass. This basket is made of willow branches. These types of baskets could also be made with red bud - "kadaadihpul" (kah-dah-dee-pull), sourberry, and small cotton wood twigs. Split willow and sourberry were used as twine to help weave this basket together.

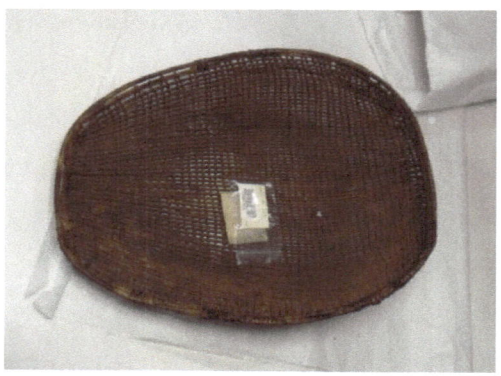

Cooking baskets - "hom'mol" (home-mole) were used to cook acorn mush. These baskets were tightly woven and may have pine pitch

rubbed on the outside and bottom portion of the basket. This would help to keep the basket from leaking. Cooking baskets were not placed upon fire. Cooking rocks were

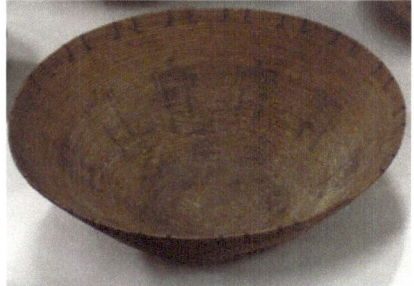

placed on an open fire and one-by-one these rocks were rotated in-out of the basket until the water or mush was boiling. Basket cooking was very common among many California Indian Tribes.

Cooking Basket   Cooking Rocks

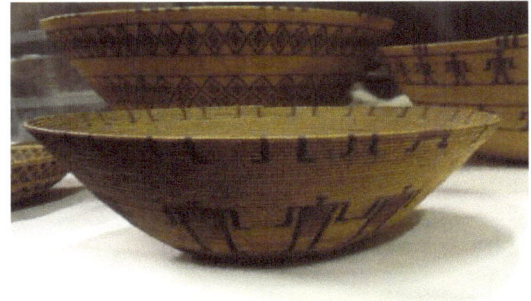   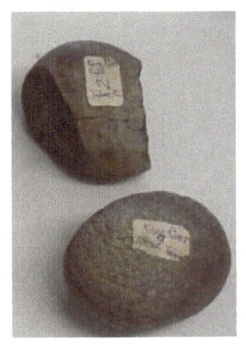

In 2009, the Alf Museum had returned a pestle rock, motor rock bowl, and two cooking rocks to the Tübatulabal Tribe through the federal law – Native American Graves Project and Repatriation Act. Picture above are the two cooking rocks that were found near "Bull Run" located on the North Fork of Kern River in the mid 1900's.

Burden Caps - "waaniht" (waa-neet) were used for both working and in ceremonies. A burden cap would be worn on the head and a strong strap "tumpline" would be placed along the top of the burden cap and connect to the bundle of wood on the back. The burden cap helped to protect the head area from the tumpline used to haul wood. This burden cap's sides are worn and faded due to the rubbing of bundle strap. The inside of the cap is faded due to the individual's head and sweat. This basket is made of deer-grass – "masil" (ma-seal), bracken-fern root, red bud, and yucca root.

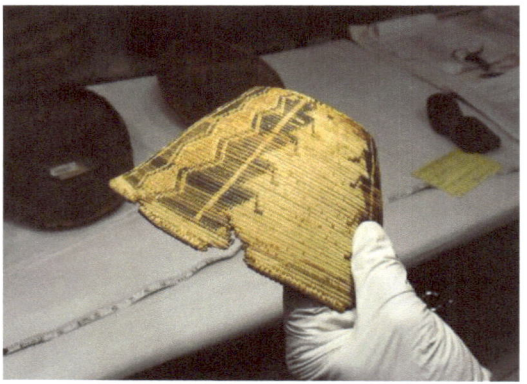

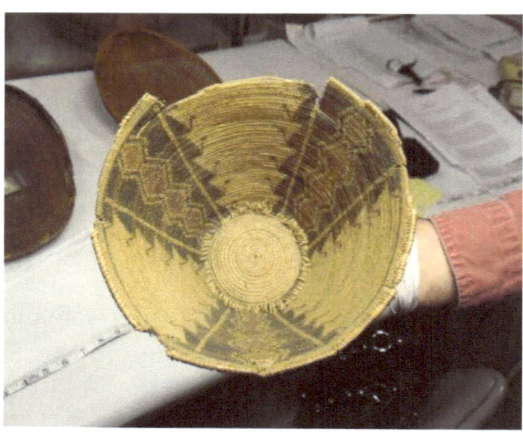

Tübatulabal Ceremonial Baskets

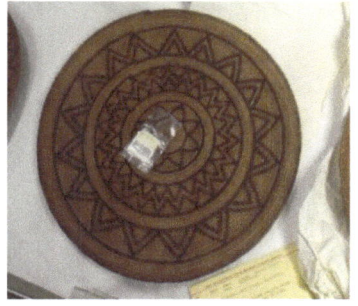

The Tübatulabals used large flat basket "waat" (waht) during their "big time" or fiestas community gatherings. These baskets were used to place food or gifts.

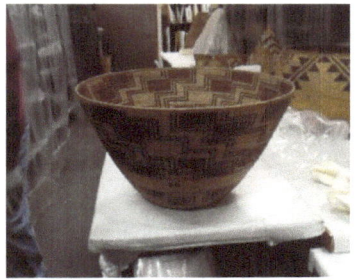

Large storage or carrying baskets were also used in ceremonies to hold acorns, piñon nuts, fruit, tobacco, and other native foods.

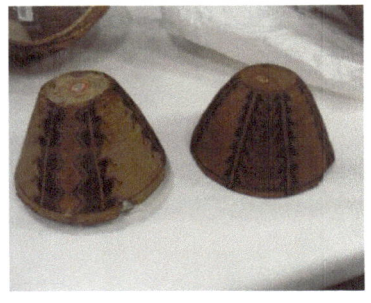

The burden caps were also worn at special events or ceremonies (Left burden cap was for work and right burden basket for special ceremonial events).

Tübatulabal Basket Designs and Materials

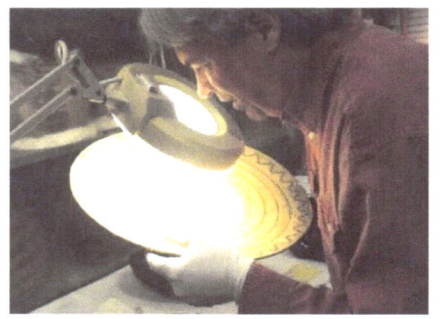

Brian Bibby exams flat basket for type of basket making materials, weaving technique, base material of the basket coil, and change in colors – what type of material used to make the color. Each basket has a computerized record of its history, type of basket, age, purpose, materials used to make the basket, tribal perspectives, and other information. Today, it is very important for Tribes to interpret and discuss the meaning of their basket designs. Many Tribal Basket Makers are Elders who can share their traditional knowledge of the basket designs and weaving methods. This traditional knowledge can be saved and shared for future generations.

The Tübatulabals shared symmetrical designs with the Shoshone Paiutes and Kawaiisu Tribes for their flat basket design pictured below.

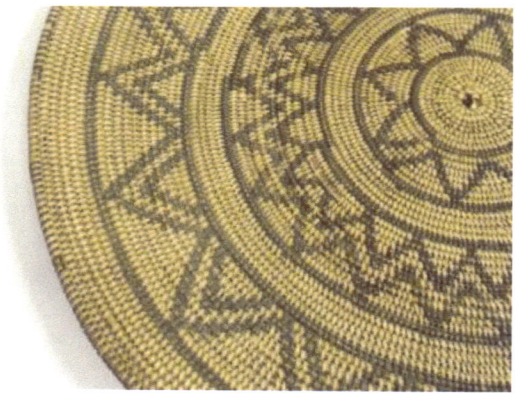

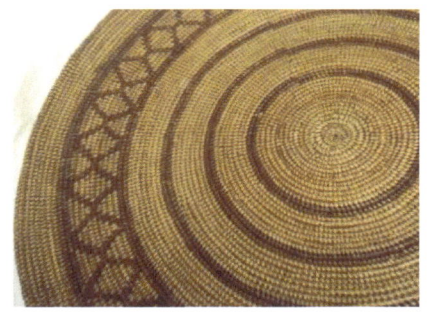

Another example of flat basket design – with symmetrical design.

Below, a large gathering or storage basket has deer hoof - "culunt tohiil" (shu-lunt toe-hill) design.

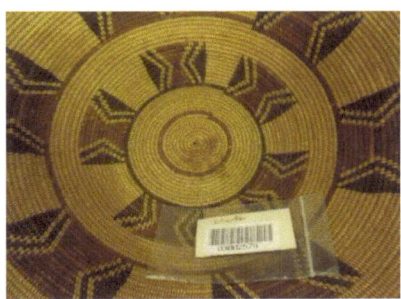

Individual pattern is deer hoof (pictured left) and collectively (same basket picture below), the entire basket is representing "deer trails" – which provide good hunting and travel routes.

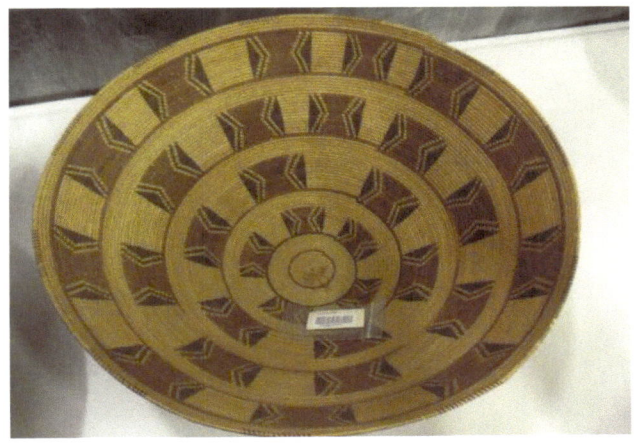

Below, is quail - "takaah" (ta-kah) pattern and collectively, the basket reflects "quails in the valley". In Kern Valley there is a very unique eco-system that provides excellent habitat for the quails, golden eagles, red-tail hawks, humming birds, blue jays, falcons, ravens, turkey vultures, California Condor, and many other bird species (visit Audubon Kern River Preserve web site: www.kern.audubon.org for more information about Kern Valley area birds).

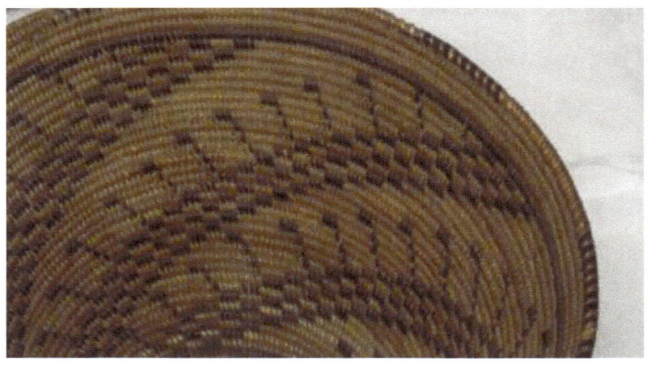

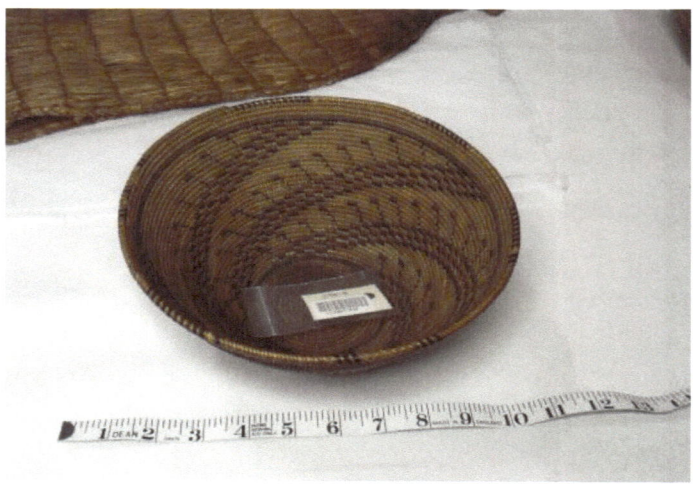

Below is little boy - "anaihiiloowun" (an-eye-he-low-wun) pattern – notice the hands are not touching. Also, the Tübatulabal common number is three - "pai" (pie). Three stitch marks are often found on the rim of our baskets. Individual design reflects people in a circle.

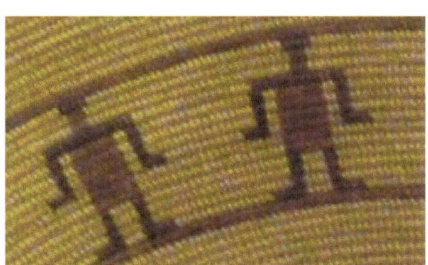
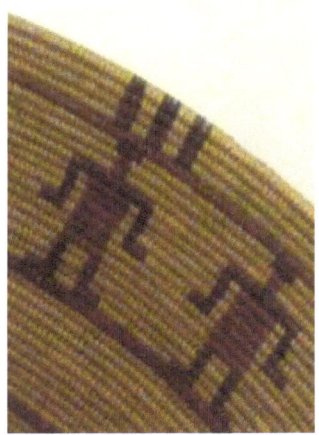

Overall, basket design reflects a community basket with spirits in the middle of the basket.

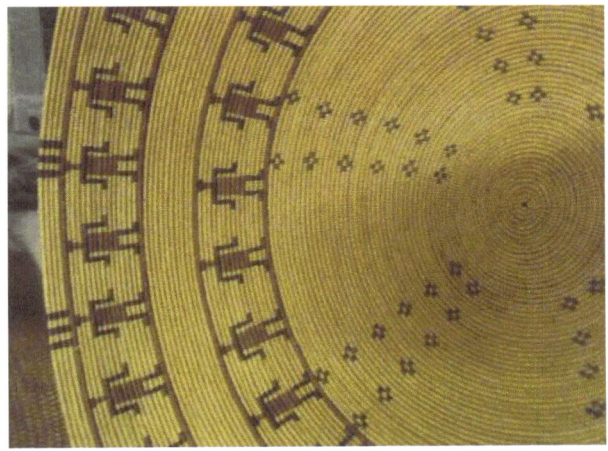

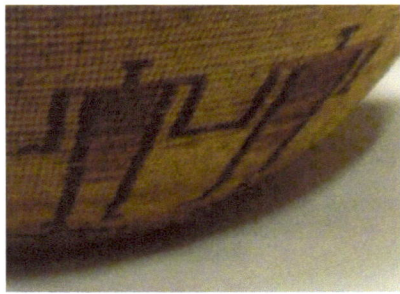

People holding hands pattern are very common on our cooking baskets and ceremonial baskets.

Individual pattern reflects thunder - "dawaagalanggil" (da-wog-ga-long-ill). Collectively, the basket represents storm pattern.

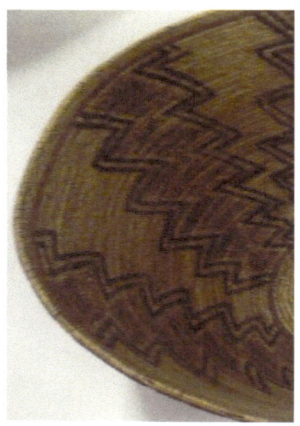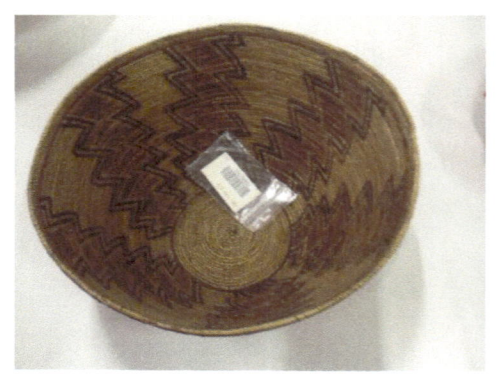

The Tübatulabals are known for their rain making ceremonies and often called to assist California Central Valley Tribes with water needs – per Steban Miranda (last Rain Maker).

The Tübatulabal Tribe is currently seeking their federal recognition. The proceeds for this book will help to develop compelling research support to prove our existence within the greater Kern Valley prior to 1852. Together with traditional language, baskets, archeological evidence, and on-going government-to-government support, the Tübatulabals will soon join the 110 federally recognized California Tribes. Today, there are over 50 California Tribes that are actively pursuing their federal acknowledgement.

Tübatulabal Tribe has developed "government-to-government" relationships with U.S. Forest Service – Sequoia Forest District, U.S. Bureau of Land Management – Bakersfield and Ridgecrest, U.S. Indian Health Services – California Area Office, U.S. Bureau of Indian Affairs – Lake Isabella, U.S. Corps of Engineers, California Native American Heritage Commission, and Kern County to continue to access traditional territories, gather traditional basket materials and native foods and medicines, conduct traditional ceremonies, and provide guidance of natural resources and land stewardship. Both Tule River Indian Reservation and Tachi Yokuts of Santa Rosa Rancheria provide support for the Tübatulabal Tribe's ability to participate in the federal NAGPRA process and consultation process with federal and state agencies.

We hope that you enjoy reading about the Tübatulabal Tribal history, paka'anil dialect, basket makers' history, and basket uses and design. Our Tribe is one of the 63 aboriginal Tribes of California. Our Tribal Government Office and Pakanapul Language Program are located in Mountain Mesa, CA (about 1 hour east of Bakersfield, CA).

References

Bibby, Brian. (2009) Overview of Tübatulabal's baskets at California State Parks Museum Resource Center – verbal description and on-site visit by the Tübatulabal Tribe. November 2009.

Bibby, Brian. (2010) Email response to Donna Miranda-Begay that describes Hall-Sheedy basket collection travels and when these baskets were donated to California State Parks.

Gomez, Robert. (2009) Tübatulabal History Outline – report for California Tribal Environmental Justice Collaborative Grant Project. September, 2010.

Macri, Marta, PhD. (2009) *Native California Languages of the San Joaquin Valley.* UC Davis. December, 2009 – report prepared for the California Tribal Environmental Justice Collaborative Grant Project.

Otay, William (2009). Oral Kern Valley history as told to Donna Miranda-Begay in 2009 at Marie Bovey's home in San Jose, CA.

Pakanapul Language Program (2010). Paka'anil dialect – basket related words.

Theodoratus, Dorothea, PhD. and McBride, Kathleen (2009). *"California Tribal Environmental Justice Collaborative Grant Project"* - report for California Tribal Environmental Justice Collaborative Grant Project. November, 2010.

Smith, Charles R. 1978. Tübatulabal. *Handbook of North American Indians*, Volume 8, California, pp. 437-445, William C. Sturtevant, general editor, and Robert F. Heizer, volume editor. Washington, DC: Smithsonian Institution Press.

Waterman, Thomas Talbot (nd; 1885-1936). *Tübatulabal texts, vocabulary, and ethnographic notes*. Berkeley, CA: Ethnological Documents of the Department and Museum of Anthropology, University of California, Berkeley, 1875-1958.

Wheeler-Voegelin, Erminie (1938). *Tübatulabal Ethnography*. Berkeley, CA: University of California Press.

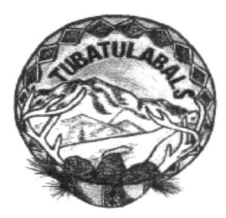

Tübatulabal Tribe
P.O. Box 226
Lake Isabella, CA 93240
Tübatulabal Tribal Office (760) 379-4590

Pakanapul Language Program (760) 379-5220

Tribal Web Site:
www.tubat.org

ISBN-13: 978-1467996365
ISBN-10: 146799636X